CONTEMPORARY POLISH POSTERS
in Full Color

Selected and Introduced by

JOSEPH S. CZESTOCHOWSKI

EXECUTIVE DIRECTOR
CEDAR RAPIDS ART CENTER, CEDAR RAPIDS, IOWA

in cooperation with

JANINA FIJAŁKOWSKA

CURATOR, MUZEUM PLAKATU (POSTER MUSEUM), WILANÓW

DOVER PUBLICATIONS, INC.
NEW YORK

ACKNOWLEDGMENTS

This publication is the combined effort of several individuals and institutions. The original impetus was provided by a research grant to the Maryland Institute, College of Art (Baltimore) from the Smithsonian Institution Foreign Currency Program. Subsequent support was provided by the Polish Ministry of Culture and Fine Arts, and the National Museum in Warsaw. This culminated in the organization of an exhibit of 180 posters, which after opening in Baltimore in 1978, is to tour the United States for two years. For their kind consideration in this endeavor, I would like to thank the following individuals: S. Dillon Ripley, Francine Berkowitz, Reggie Lipsky, Theodore Klitzke, John Slorp, Cyril Satorsky, The Honorable Barbara Mikulski, The Honorable John Brademas, Frank Sullivan Jr., Janina Fijałkowska, Peter Becskehazy, Zdzisław Kozłowicz, Krystyna Orchowska and Janusz Przewoźny. Above all, I am grateful to His Excellency Romuald Spasowski, Ambassador of the Polish People's Republic, for his gracious patronage of this exhibit and publication. Finally, I would like to thank Hayward Cirker, President of Dover Publications, for recognizing the merit of this project and for furthering cultural exchange between Poland and the United States.

I completed the work on the present volume while Director of the Decker Gallery of the Maryland Institute, College of Art.

JOSEPH S. CZESTOCHOWSKI

Front cover. **Jan Lenica:** the opera *Don Giovanni* (1975)
Inside front cover. **Waldemar Świerzy:** circus (1975)
Inside back cover. **Robert Knuth:** the musical *Reanimation* (1976)
Back cover. **Hubert Hilscher:** circus (1970)

Copyright © 1979 by Dover Publications, Inc.
All rights reserved under Pan American and International Copyright Conventions.

Published in Canada by General Publishing Company, Ltd., 30 Lesmill Road, Don Mills, Toronto, Ontario.

Published in the United Kingdom by Constable and Company, Ltd., 10 Orange Street, London WC2H 7EG.

Contemporary Polish Posters in Full Color is a new work, first published by Dover Publications, Inc., in 1979.

Editor and publisher are grateful to the Muzeum Plakatu at Wilanów, Poland, for making the original posters available for reproduction.

International Standard Book Number: 0-486-23780-X
Library of Congress Catalog Card Number: 78-64945

Manufactured in the United States of America
Dover Publications, Inc.
180 Varick Street
New York, N.Y. 10014

Introduction

Polish posters have achieved singular distinction in the past twenty years. Gradually they have evolved from a rather traditional interpretation to an innovative and refreshing graphic statement. Almost immediately, their imagery transcended national boundaries and attained international acclaim. Although these posters have been exhibited extensively throughout Europe, they are rarely presented either to the American public or to the many students of graphic design in this country.

The current collection is a survey of the most important cultural posters of recent years (1961–77). Selected from the world's first museum devoted exclusively to poster art, the Muzeum Plakatu at Wilanów near Warsaw, these works document the outstanding achievement of contemporary Polish designers. Finally, this publication follows not long after Warsaw's 1978 hosting of the Seventh International Poster Biennale, an event that in itself acknowledges Poland's contribution to this art form.

Polish poster art became an organized movement between 1890 and 1905 in the ateliers of several great painters. Its participants included Stanisław Wyspiański (1869–1907), Józef Mehoffer (1869–1946), Teodor Axentowicz (1859–1938) and Wojciech Weiss (1875–1950). Cousin to European Art Nouveau and intimately connected with the resurging interest in Polish folk art, these earliest posters were characterized by decorative color patterns and a rhythmic flow of line. From the outset, their distinctiveness was recognized by critics in Paris, Vienna and Munich.

Between 1919 and 1939, Polish designers assembled a rich repertoire of visual images. They continued to respond with sensitivity to the experiments of the numerous European art movements—Cubism, Constructivism, Futurism and Surrealism. Increasingly, their ranks attracted individuals from disciplines other than applied graphic design. Among others, these disciplines included printmaking, painting, architecture, sculpture and cinematography.

In order to fully appreciate the modern Polish poster, it is necessary to understand its role in the recovery of Polish cultural life following the devastating Second World War. Working within a totally state-supported artistic system, Polish designers assumed one of the most important positions in the reconstruction of a viable social psychology. Their immediate problem was to reconcile the autonomous aims of art, beauty and aesthetics with the realistic demands of an emerging state. The solution was not an easy one, since works from the 1950s were characterized by both an extremely didactic approach and a hard, architectonic quality of line. By the beginning of the 1960s, the stylistic innovations of Henryk Tomaszewski and Tadeusz Trepkowski prompted a new attitude and approach. The earlier label of a uniform "Polish school of posters" became outdated as a diversity of individual expressions prevailed. Also, Polish society gradually began to regard poster design as an art form equal in importance to painting.

As might be expected, contemporary Polish posters have little to do with advertising in the Western sense. Only recently has this imagery been applied to tourism and rarely does it reflect political opinions. Rather, it is applied to themes of a social nature (health, the environment) and, much more frequently, to themes of a cultural nature (the circus, national celebrations, education, films, theater performances, music and sports events, and artistic exhibitions). The circus posters, an ongoing series, are not related to specific troupes or performances.

For several years, critics have been able to detect the emergence of a new "intellectual" genre in the art of the poster. This genre operates on the frontier of both the conceptual vision of optic painting and of visual communication through functional typography.

Many of the younger poster designers, such as Jan Jaromir Aleksiun, Jerzy Czerniawski, Jan Sawka and Eugeniusz Stankiewicz, are also working as painters, printmakers and cinematographers. This situation has caused a particularly interesting phenomenon, namely the reconciliation of the modern poster and the so-called free disciplines. On a visit to Warsaw, this writer was startled by the sudden appearance of a recently installed sculpture display. Located on the sidewalks on both sides of a busy street, the sculpture depicted a gradually descending figural group and on the other side, a similar group of figures ascending from the ground. Passersby were at once surprised and intrigued. When inquiries were made, it was revealed that students in poster design were experimenting with alternative ways of expressing their visual metaphors. This current trend should have a profound effect on both the development of the poster's visual language and the diffusion and adoption of its imagery in the West.

JOSEPH S. CZESTOCHOWSKI

The Artists and the Posters

Jan Jaromir Aleksiun. Born 1940 in Nowa Wilejka. Attended the Academy of Fine Arts in Wrocław, where he is now an assistant professor. Awards: Cracow (Kraków), 1970; Lugano, 1972; Warsaw (Warszawa), 1974. **Plate 1:** *Anna Livia* (1977), play by Maciej Słomczyński adapted from works by James Joyce, at the Contemporary Theater (Teatr Współczesny), Wrocław; 96 × 67 cm; published by the theater; printed by the State Graphic Workshops (Państwowe Zakłady Graficzne), Wrocław.

Roman Cieślewicz. Born 1930 in Lvov (Ukraine). Attended the Academy of Fine Arts, Cracow. Since 1963, lecturer at the Ecole Nationale Supérieure des Arts Décoratifs, Paris. Has won 40 prizes. **Plate 2:** *The Prisoner* [Il Prigioniero] (1962), opera by Luigi Dallapiccola, at the Warsaw Opera; 95 × 66.7 cm; published by the Opera; printed by the Capital-City Printshops (Stołeczne Zakłady Drukarskie No. 4), Warsaw. **Plate 3:** *"Che" Si* (1967), abstract portrait of Che Guevara, from the series of Opus posters commissioned by the Parisian journal *Opus International*; 81 × 55 cm; published by Georges Fall, Paris; printed by S.E.R.G., Paris.

Jerzy Czerniawski. Born 1947 in Kwiatow. Attended the Academy of Fine Arts, Wrocław. Awards: Warsaw, 1974; Cagnes-sur-Mer, 1976. **Plate 4:** *A Study of Hamlet* (1975), design commissioned by the Teatr Ateneum, Warsaw; 66.5 × 98 cm; published by the Foreign Trade Enterprise "Desa," Warsaw; printed by the Job-Printing House (Drukarnia Akcydensowa), Warsaw. **Plate 5:** *Ballets by Birgit Cullberg* (1975), for works staged for the Swedish choreographer at the Big Theater (Teatr Wielki), Warsaw; 97.5 × 66.5 cm; published by the theater; printed by the Job-Printing House, Warsaw. **Plate 6:** *Circus* (1975); 97.5 × 67.5; published by the United Entertainment Enterprise (Zjednoczone Przedsiębiorstwo Rozrykowe), Warsaw; printed by the State Graphic Workshops, Bydgoszcz. **Plate 7:** *Pan* [Mr.] *Jowialski* (1977), classic 19th-century comedy by Aleksander Fredro, at the Contemporary Theater, Warsaw; 97.5 × 66.5 cm; published by the theater; printed by the Job-Printing House, Warsaw. The couplet reads: "The man who seeks truth is heading for trouble."

Hubert Hilscher. Born 1924 in Warsaw. Attended the Academy of Fine Arts there. Art director of the magazine *Projekt*. Numerous awards. **Back cover:** *Circus* (1970), from the series commissioned by "Desa"; 68.5 × 98.5 cm; published by the United Entertainment Enterprise, Warsaw; printed by the State Graphic Workshops, Workers' Publishing Cooperative (RSW) "Prasa" ["Press"], Bydgoszcz. **Plate 8:** *Circus* (1970), from series for "Desa"; 99 × 67 cm; published by the United Entertainment Enterprise, Warsaw; printed by

"Prasa," Bydgoszcz. **Plate 9:** *Circus* (1974), from series for "Desa"; 97 × 66.5 cm; published by the United Entertainment Enterprise, Warsaw; printed by "Prasa," Bydgoszcz. **Plate 10:** *Visual Art and Design* (1974), advertising poster for *Projekt*; 67 × 98 cm; published by the KAW publishers, Warsaw; printed by "Prasa," Bydgoszcz.

Robert Knuth. Born 1952 in Bydgoszcz. Attended the Academy of Fine Arts in Gdańsk. **Inside back cover:** *Reanimation* (1976), musical with music by Józef Skrzek and words by Agnieszka Osiecka, at the Baltic Opera, Gdańsk; printed by the Graphic Workshops, Gdańsk.

Jan Lenica. Born 1928 in Poznań. Attended the Technical University in Warsaw. Also a cartoonist and animator. Awards: Versailles, 1961; Warsaw, 1966 (gold medal for *Wozzeck*); Oberhausen, 1966. **Plate 11:** *Wozzeck* (1966), opera by Alban Berg, at the Teatr Wielki, Warsaw; 95.5 × 67 cm; published by the theater; printed by the Capital-City Graphic Workshops (Stołeczne Zakłady Graficzne No. 2), Warsaw. **Plate 12:** *Variations on a Theme by Purcell* (1964), ballet by Benjamin Britten, at the Teatr Wielki in Łódź, from the series commissioned by "Desa"; 97.5 × 67 cm; published by the theater, 1971; printed by "Prasa," Bydgoszcz. **Plate 13:** *Poland Invites You* (1970), tourist poster published in five languages; 95.5 × 67 cm; published by the Polish Tourist Information Centre, Warsaw; printed by "Prasa," Bydgoszcz. **Plate 14:** *Fantazy* (1973), play by 19th-century poet Juliusz Słowacki, at the Teatr Ateneum, Warsaw; 94 × 67 cm; published by the theater; printed by the State Graphic Workshops, Workers' Publishing Cooperative "Prasa-Książka-Ruch" ["Press-Book-Action"], Wrocław. **Front cover:** *Don Giovanni* (1975), opera by Wolfgang Amadeus Mozart, at the Teatr Wielki, Warsaw; 96 × 66 cm; published by the theater; printed by the Job-Printing House, Warsaw. **Plate 15:** *6th International Poster Biennale Warsaw 1976* (1975); 97 × 66 cm; published by the Central Office for Art Exhibitions, Warsaw; printed by the Job-Printing House No. 3, Warsaw. **Plate 16:** *Phèdre* (1977), classic French play by Jean Racine, at the Little Theater (Teatr Mały), Warsaw; 96 × 65.5 cm; published by the National Theater (Teatr Narodowy), Warsaw; printed by the Job-Printing House, Warsaw.

Jan Młodożeniec. Born 1929 in Warsaw. Attended the Academy of Fine Arts there. Awards: Vienna, 1955; Leipzig, 1965; Brno, 1966. **Plate 17:** *I Pagliacci* (1974), opera by Ruggiero Leoncavallo, at the State [Państwowa] Opera in Wrocław; 98 × 66.5 cm; published by the Opera; printed by the Cartographic Printshop (Drukarnia Kartograficzna), Wrocław.

Józef Mroszczak. Born 1910 in Nowy Targ, died 1975 in Warsaw. Attended the Schools of Applied Art in Cracow and Vienna. Taught at the Academy of Fine Arts in Warsaw. Awards: Zurich, 1968; Brno, 1974. **Plate 18:** *Boris Godunov* (1961), opera by Modest Mussorgski, commissioned by the State Opera in Warsaw; 97.5 × 67; published by the Artistic Graphic Publishing House (Wydawnictwo Artystyczno-Graficzne), Warsaw, 1969; printed by the State Graphic Workshops, Workers' Publishing Cooperative "Prasa" in Łódź. **Plate 19:** *Coppélia* (1975), ballet by Léo Delibes; 97 × 67.5 cm; published by "Desa," Warsaw; printed by the Zakład [Workshop] Poligraficzny "AGPOL," Warsaw.

Julian Pałka. Born 1923 in Poznań. Attended the Academy of Fine Arts in Warsaw, where he now teaches. Awards: Warsaw, 1968; Sofia, 1968. **Plate 20:** *Romeo and Juliet* (1970), ballet by Sergei Prokofiev, at the Teatr Wielki in Warsaw; 98 × 65.5 cm; published by the theater; printed by the Job-Printing House No. 2, Warsaw.

Andrzej Pągowski. Born 1953 in Warsaw. Student at the Academy of Fine Arts in Poznań. **Plate 21:** *Husband and Wife* (1977), 19th-century comedy by Aleksander Fredro, at the Teatr Mały, Warsaw; 96 × 67; published by the National Theater, Warsaw; printed by the State Graphic Workshops, Wrocław. **Plate 22:** *Świerzy* (1977), portrait of poster artist Waldemar Świerzy (see pages 30–35 and inside front cover), with allusions to his style; 93.5 × 67 cm; published by the National Theater, Warsaw; printed by the Job-Printing House No. 2, Warsaw. **Plate 23:** *F. Starowieyski* (1977), portrait of poster artist Franciszek Starowieyski (see pages 26–29), with allusions to his style; 91.5 × 65; published by the National Theater, Warsaw; printed by the Job-Printing House No. 2, Warsaw.

Jan Sawka. Born 1946 in Zabrze. Attended the Technical University and the Academy of Fine Arts in Wrocław. Award: Cagnes-sur-Mer, 1975. **Plate 24:** *Circus* (1973); 95 × 67 cm; published by the United Entertainment Enterprise, Warsaw, 1974; printed by the State Graphic Workshops, Workers' Publishing Cooperative "Prasa-Książka-Ruch" in Katowice. **Plate 25:** *Buffalo Bill* (1975), play by Arthur Kopit, at the General Theater (Teatr Powszechny), Warsaw; 97.5 × 67.5 cm; published by the theater; printed by the Printshop of the Publishing Institute (Drukarnia Instytutu Wydawniczego), Central Workers' Sales Agency (CRZZ), Warsaw.

Franciszek Starowieyski. Born 1930 in Cracow. Attended the Academy of Fine Arts there. Awards: Warsaw, 1974; Los Angeles, 1976; Cannes, 1976. **Plate 26:** *The Lover* and *A Slight Ache* (1970), two plays by Harold Pinter, at the Experimental Division of the Dramatic Theater, Warsaw; 83.5 × 59; published by the theater; printed by the Military [Wojskowe] Graphic Workshops, Warsaw. **Plate 27:** *Illumination* (1973), film directed by Krzysztof Zanussi; 80.5 × 57.5 cm; published by the Film Distribution Office (Centrala Wynajmu Filmów), Warsaw; printed by the Lublin [Lubelskie] Graphic Workshops, Lublin. Additional text on poster: (left side) "In the principal roles: Stanisław Latałło, Małgorzata Pritulak"; (right side) "Photography: Edward Kłosiński. Pro-

duction: 'Tor.'" **Plate 28:** *The Sandglass Sanatorium* (1973), film directed by (Wojciech) J(erzy) Ha(a)s; 79.5 × 58; published by the Film Distribution Office, Warsaw; printed by the Lublin Graphic Workshops. Additional text: (top) "Award-winning film, International Film Festival, Cannes. Based on writings by Bruno Schulz"; (bottom) "Photography: Witold Sobociński. Production: 'Silesia' Collective"; (sides) "Players: Jan Nowicki, Tadeusz Kondrat, Mieczysław Voit, Halina Kowalska, Gustaw Holoubek." **Plate 29:** *The Wedding* (1975), play by Witold Gombrowicz, at the Polish Theater (Teatr Polski) in Wrocław; 94 × 66.5 cm; published by the theater; printed by the State Graphic Workshops, Wrocław. Inscription around central form: "Man is exposed to the necessity of forming himself out in the world of people and he possesses no divinity other than that which arises from that world ... here people unite in shapes like this ...."

Waldemar Świerzy. Born 1931 in Katowice. Attended the Academy of Fine Arts there. Assistant professor at the Academy of Fine Arts in Poznań. Awards: Copenhagen, 1964; Versailles, 1969; São Paulo, 1969; Warsaw, 1976; Los Angeles, 1976. **Plate 30:** *The Lady from Maxim's* [La Dame de chez Maxim's] (1968), play by Georges Feydeau, at the Variety Theater (Teatr Rozmaitości), Warsaw; 84 × 58.5 cm; published by the theater; printed by the Job-Printing House No. 2, Warsaw. **Plate 31:** *Warsaw Autumn* (1969), music festival, at the National Philharmonic Society, Warsaw; 97 × 68; published by the office of the festival; printed by the Job-Printing House No. 2, Warsaw. **Plate 32:** *Circus* (1971), from the series commissioned by "Desa"; 93 × 67.5 cm; published by the United Entertainment Enterprise, Warsaw; printed by "Prasa," Bydgoszcz. **Plate 33:** *Circus* (1972), from series commissioned by "Desa"; 98 × 67.5 cm; published by the United Entertainment Enterprise, Warsaw; printed by "Prasa," Bydgoszcz. **Plate 34:** *Jimi Hendrix* (1974), from the series "Jazz Greats"; 97.5 × 67 cm; published by the Polish Jazz Association (Polskie Stowarzyszenie Jazzowe), Warsaw; printed by "Prasa," Bydgoszcz. **Inside front cover:** *Circus* (1975), from series commissioned by "Desa"; 95.5 × 67.5 cm; published by the United Entertainment Enterprise, Warsaw; printed by the Printshops of Foreign-Trade Publications (Zakłady Drukarskie Wydawnictw Handlu Zagranicznego), Warsaw. **Plate 35:** *Circus* (1975), from "Desa" series; 97.5 × 67.5 cm; published by the United Entertainment Enterprise, Warsaw; printed by the Printshops of Foreign-Trade Publications, Warsaw.

Henryk Tomaszewski. Born 1914 in Warsaw. Attended the Academy of Fine Arts there, where he is now a professor. Awards: Vienna, 1948 (5 prizes), São Paulo, 1963; Leipzig, 1965; Warsaw, 1970. **Plate 36:** *The Belgian Secession* [Art Nouveau] *Poster* (1973), for an exhibition at the Poster Museum at Wilanów; 98.5 × 67.5 cm; published by the museum; printed by "Prasa," Bydgoszcz. Full text: "Poster Museum at Wilanów; the Belgian Secessionist poster from the collection of L. Wittamer de Camps in Brussels; June–August 1973."

Maciej Urbaniec. Born 1925 in Zwierzyniec. Attended the Academy of Fine Arts in Warsaw, where he now teaches. Awards; Brno, 1970; Kiel, 1976. **Plate 37:** *Circus* (1970); 98 × 67 cm; published by the United Entertainment Enterprise, Warsaw; printed by the State Manufacture of Stocks and Bonds (Państwowa Wytwórnia Papierów Wartościowych), Warsaw. **Plate 38:** *Boris Godunov* (1972), opera by Modest Mussorgski, at the Teatr Wielki, Warsaw; 96 × 67 cm; published by the theater; printed by the Job-Printing House No. 2, Warsaw. **Plate 39:** *International Children's Day* (1973), for the celebration on June 1, 1973; 97.5 × 66.5 cm; published by the Society of Friends of Children (Towarzystwo Przyjaciół Dzieci), Warsaw; printed by "Prasa," Bydgoszcz. **Plate 40:** *The File* (1975), play by Tadeusz Różewicz, at the Teatr Mały, Warsaw; 67.5 × 94.5 cm; published by the National Theater, Warsaw; printed by the Offset Printshops (Zakłady Offsetowe), Warsaw.

Janusz Wiktorowski. Born 1939 in Warsaw. Attended the Academy of Fine Arts in Łódź. Awards: Buenos Aires, 1966; Paris, 1968; Mannheim, 1973. **Plate 41:** *Atelier 72* (1972), for an exhibition of contemporary Polish art at the Richard Demarco Gallery in Edinburgh; 98 × 69.5 cm; published by the gallery; printed in Edinburgh.

Danuta Żukowska. Born 1932 in Łódź. Attended the Academy of Fine Arts there. Since 1967, art director of the State Publishing House for Agriculture and Forestry. **Plate 42:** *Circus* (1970); 99 × 67 cm; published by the United Entertainment Enterprise, Warsaw; printed by the Military Cartographic Workshops (Wojskowe Zakłady Kartograficzne), Warsaw.

1 Jan Jaromir Aleksiun: the play *Anna Livia* (1977)

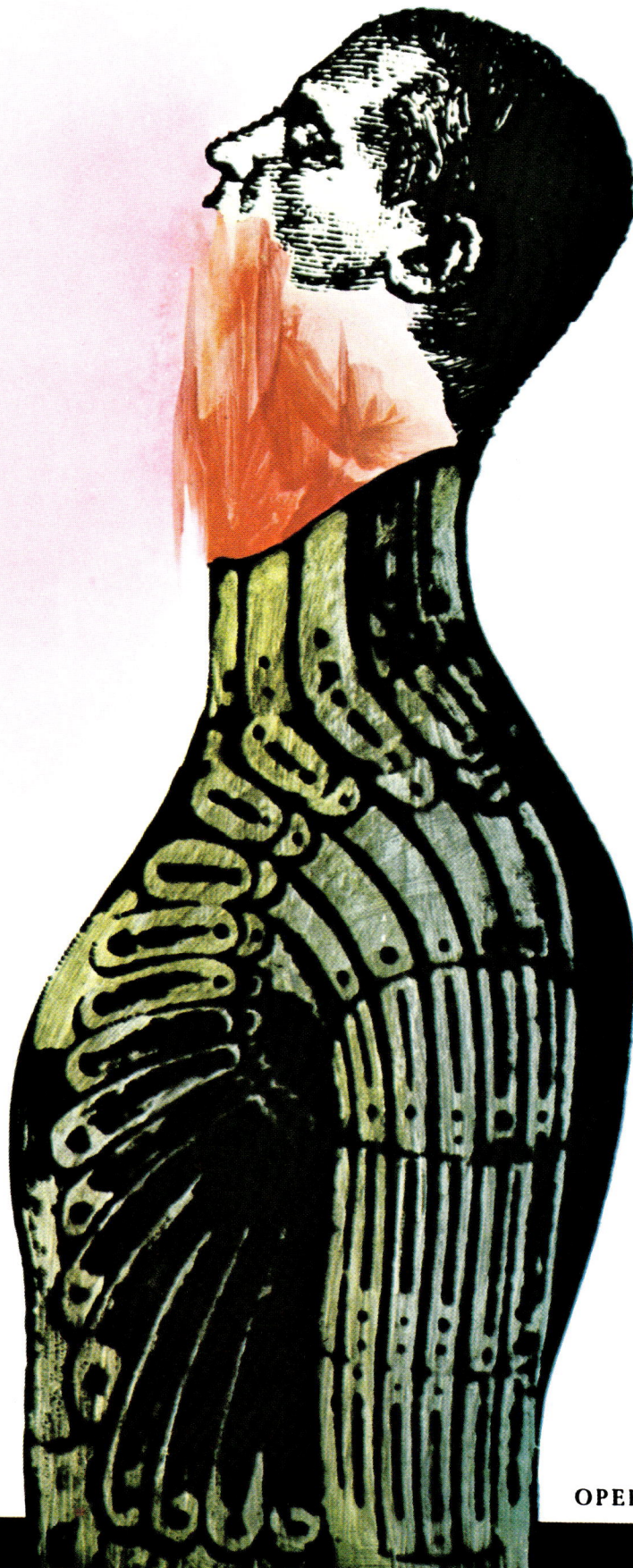

2 **Roman Cieślewicz:** the opera *The Prisoner* (1962)

3 **Roman Cieślewicz:** Che Guevara (1967)

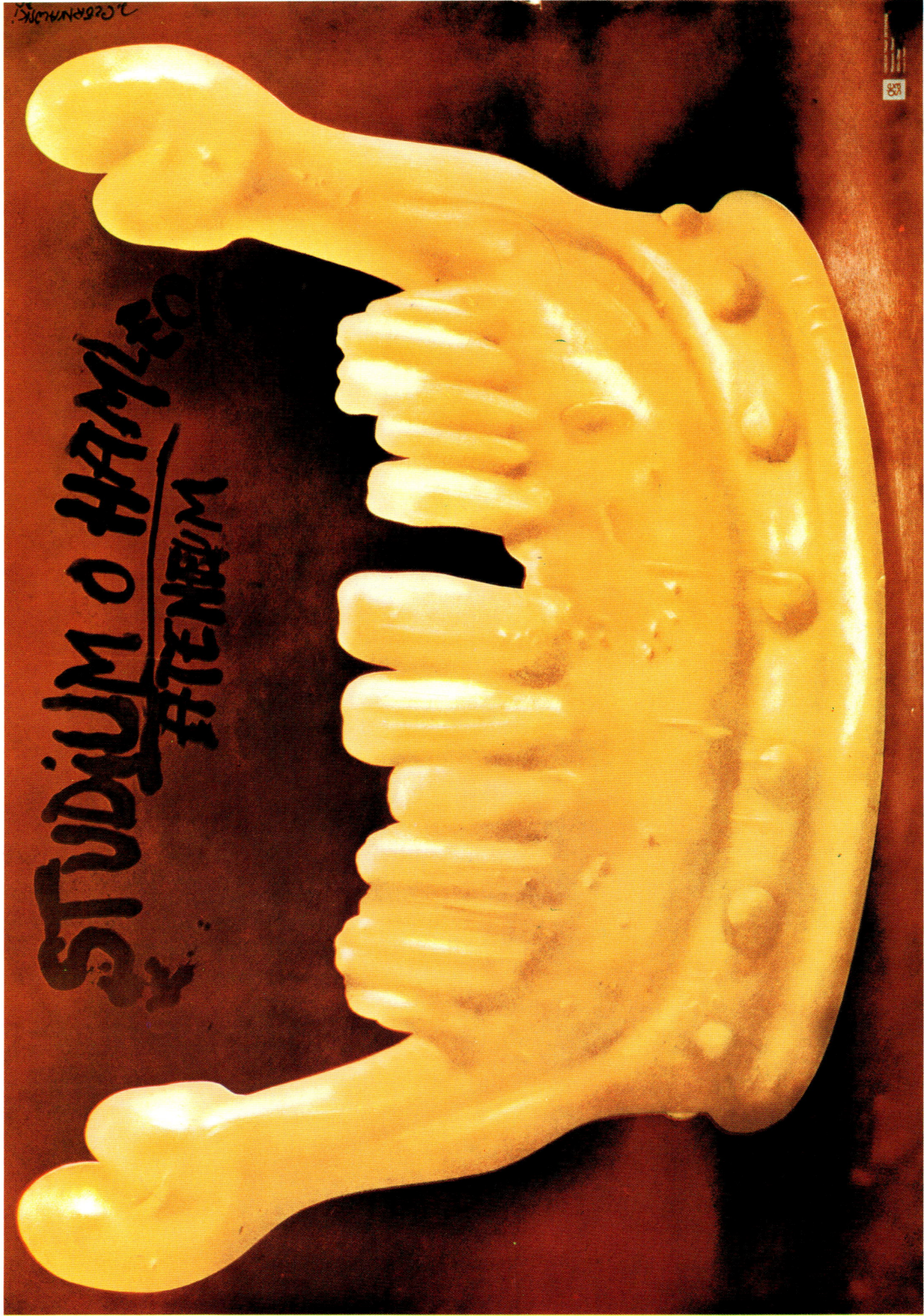

4 **Jerzy Czerniawski:** *A Study of Hamlet* (1975)

5　**Jerzy Czerniawski:** Ballets by Birgit Cullberg (1975)

6 **Jerzy Czerniawski:** circus (1975)

7 Jerzy Czerniawski: the play *Pan Jowialski* (1977)

8　**Hubert Hilscher:** circus (1970)

CYRK

9 **Hubert Hilscher:** circus (1974)

10   **Hubert Hilscher:** ad for the magazine *Projekt* (1974)

11   **Jan Lenica:** the opera *Wozzeck* (1964)

Teatr Wielki

BRITTEN   Wariacje na temat Purcella

12   **Jan Lenica:** the ballet *Variations on a Theme by Purcell* (1964)

Poland invites you

13 **Jan Lenica:** tourism poster (1970)

14 **Jan Lenica:** the play *Fantazy* (1973)

15 **Jan Lenica:** international poster show (1975)

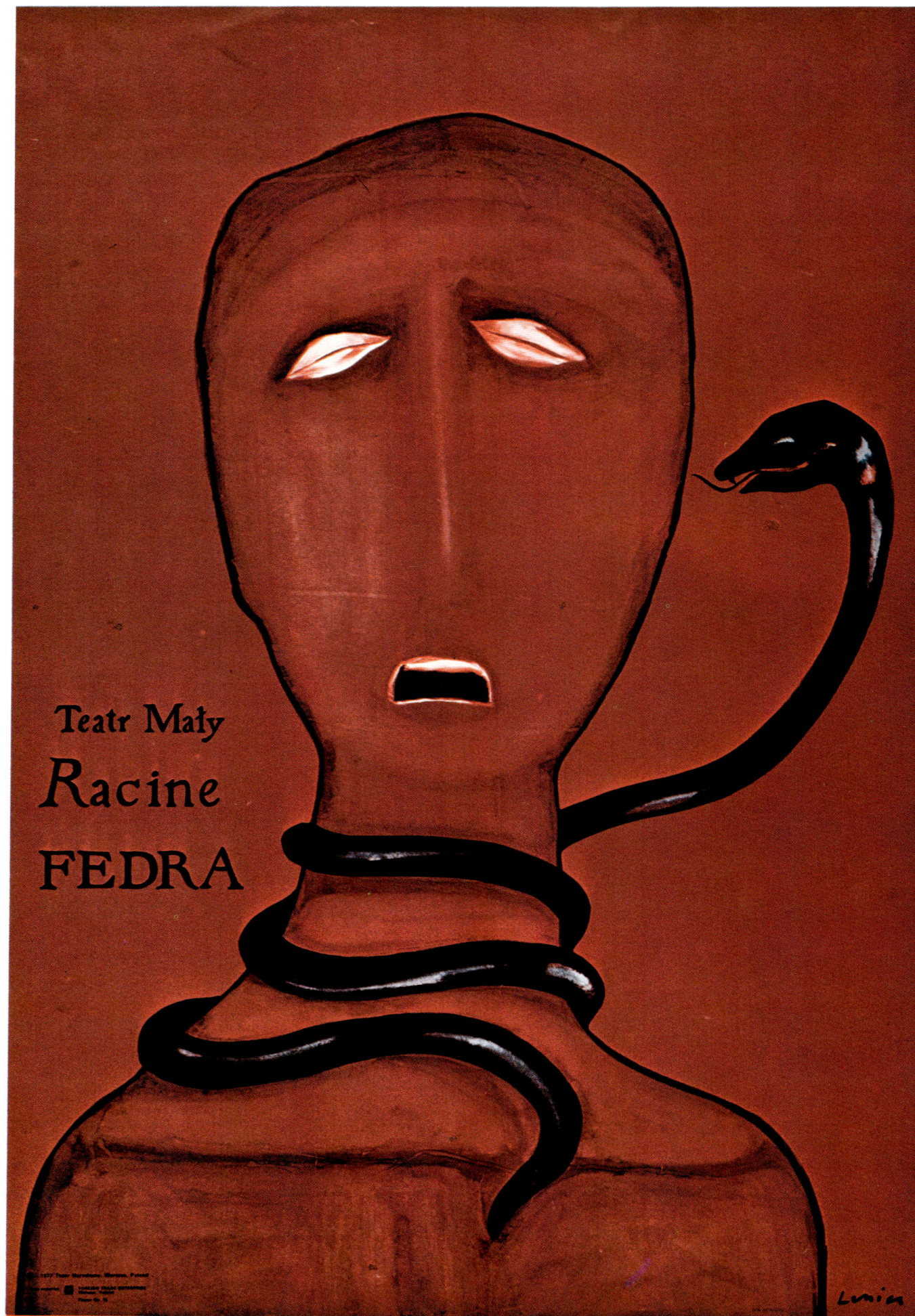

16 **Jan Lenica:** the play *Phèdre* (1977)

17 Jan Młodożeniec: the opera *I Pagliacci* (1974)

18 **Józef Mroszczak:** *the opera Boris Godunov* (1961)

19   **Józef Mroszczak:** the ballet *Coppélia* (1975)

20 **Julian Pałka:** the ballet *Romeo and Juliet* (1970)

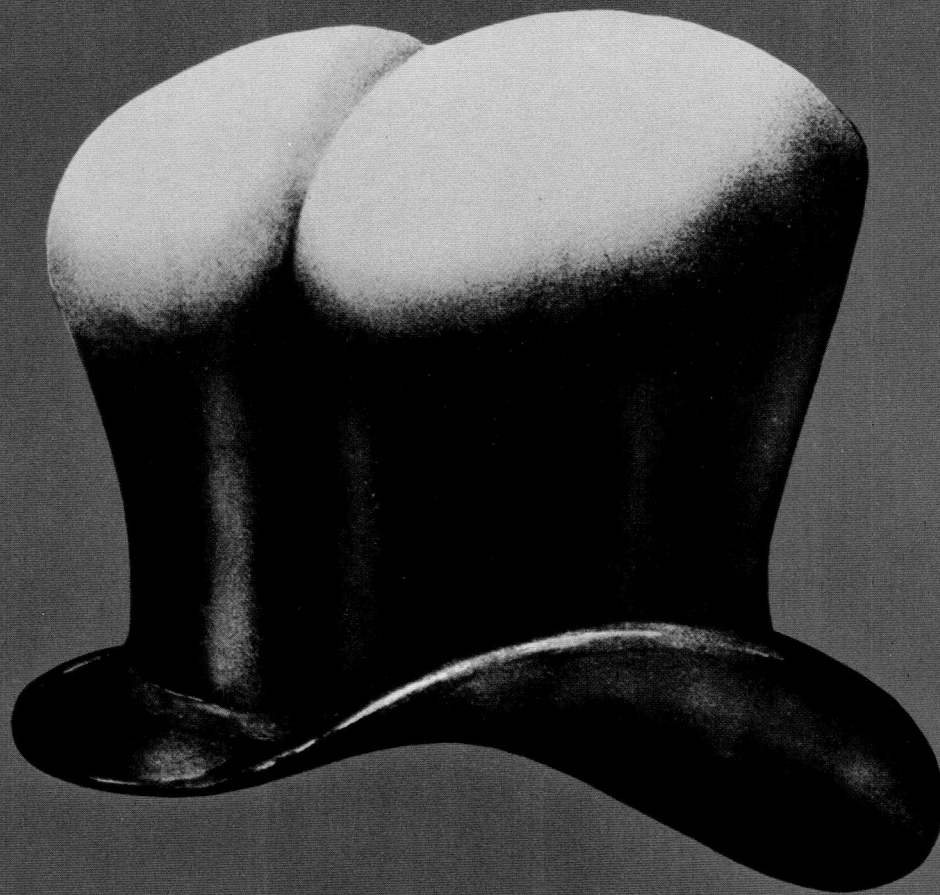

ALEKSANDER·FREDRO

mąż i żona

Husband and wife

21   **Andrzej Pągowski:** the play *Husband and Wife* (1977)

22 **Andrzej Pągowski:** portrait of Waldemar Świerzy (1977)

23 **Andrzej Pągowski:** portrait of Franciszek Starowieyski (1977)

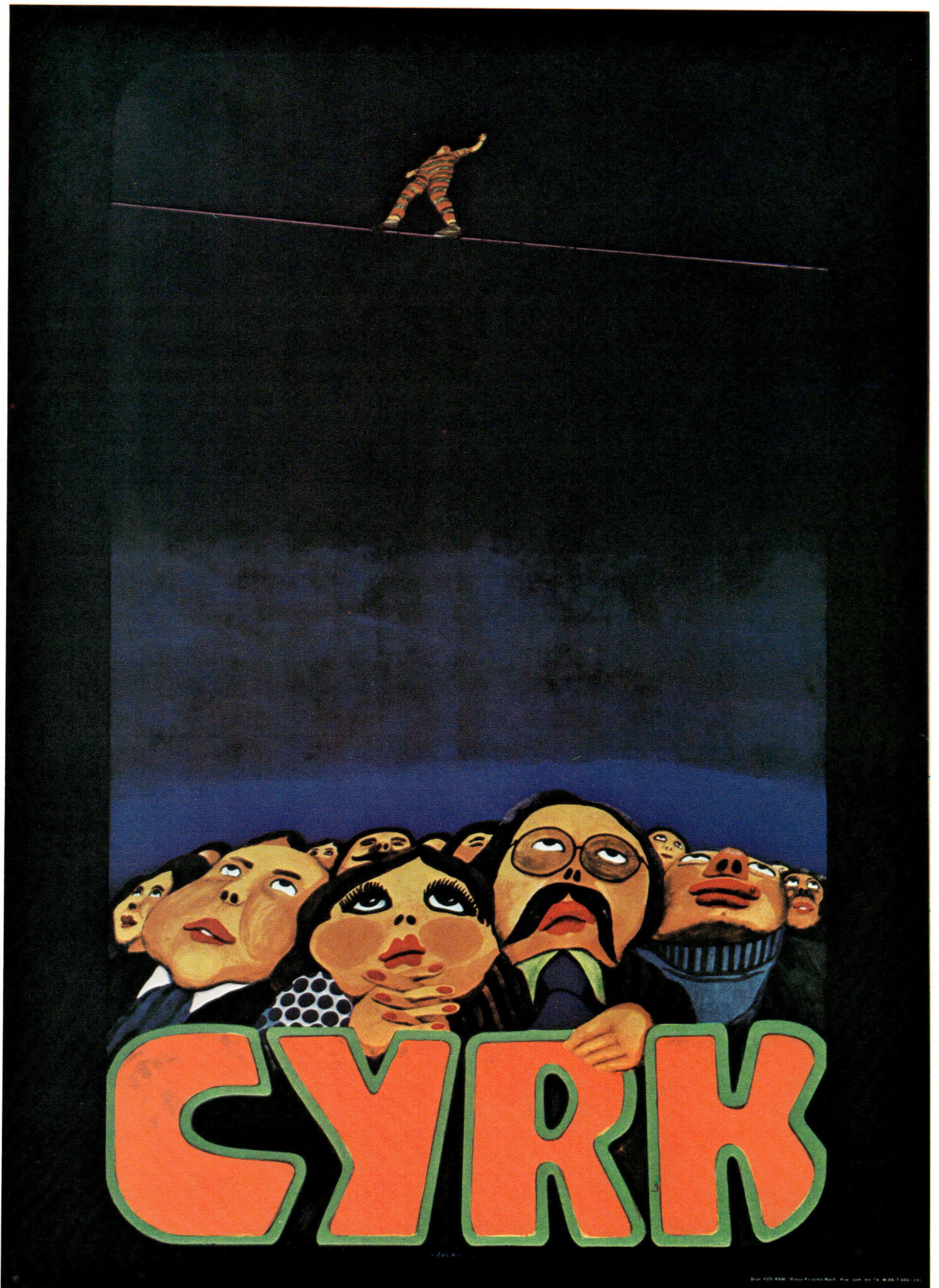

24 **Jan Sawka:** circus (1973)

25 **Jan Sawka:** the play *Buffalo Bill* (1975)

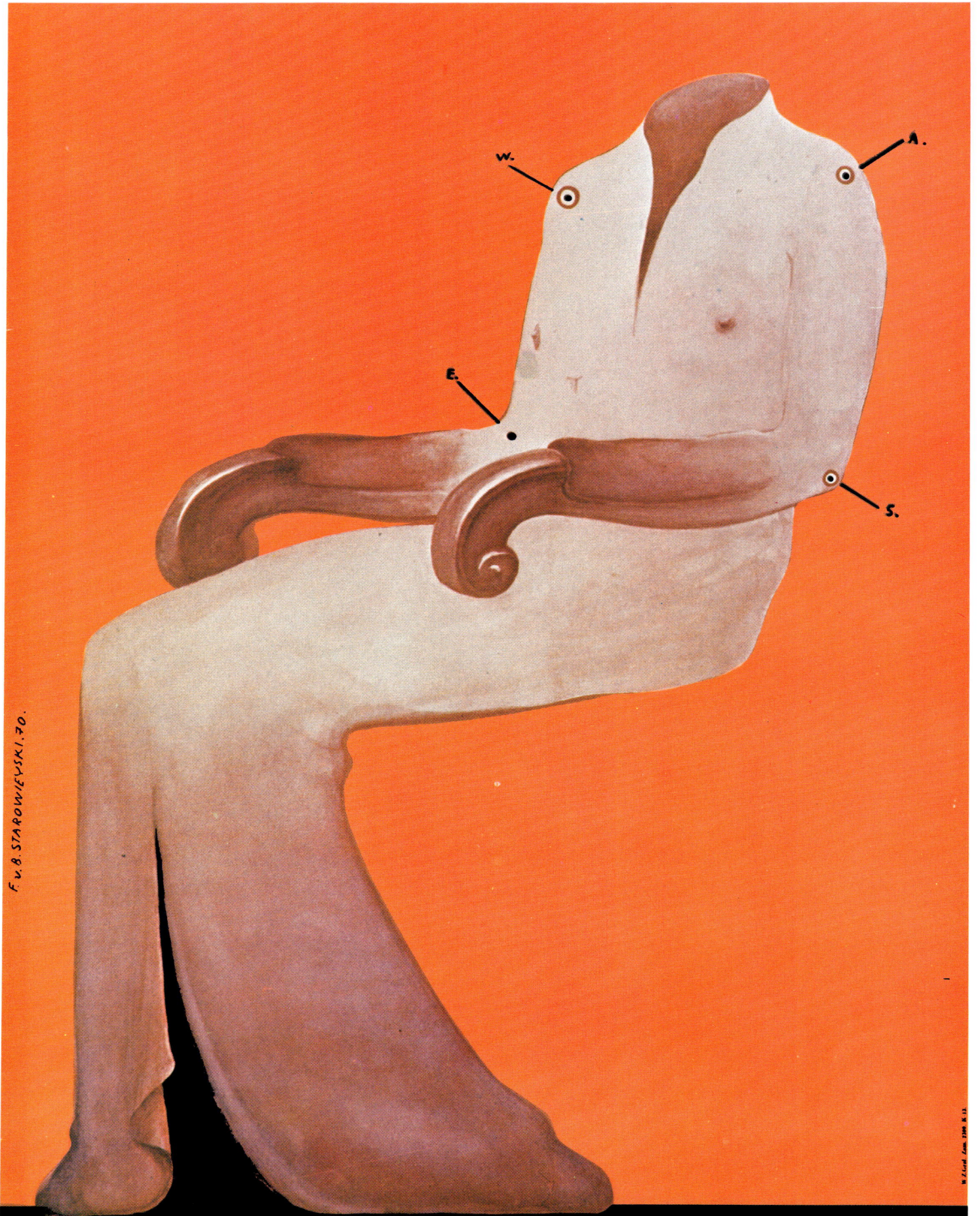

26 **Franciszek Starowieyski:** the plays *The Lover* and *A Slight Ache* (1970)

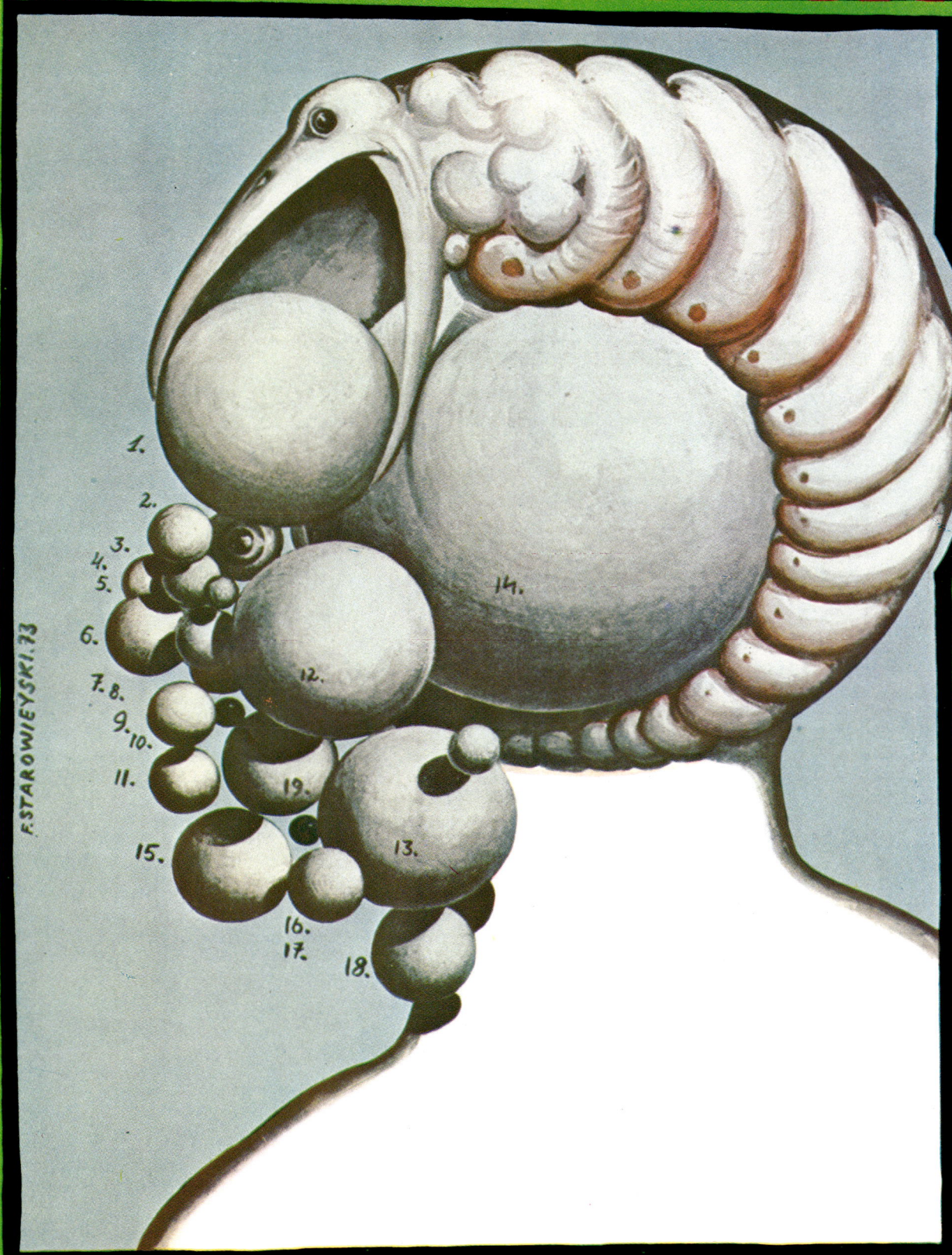

27 **Franciszek Starowieyski:** the film *Illumination* (1973)

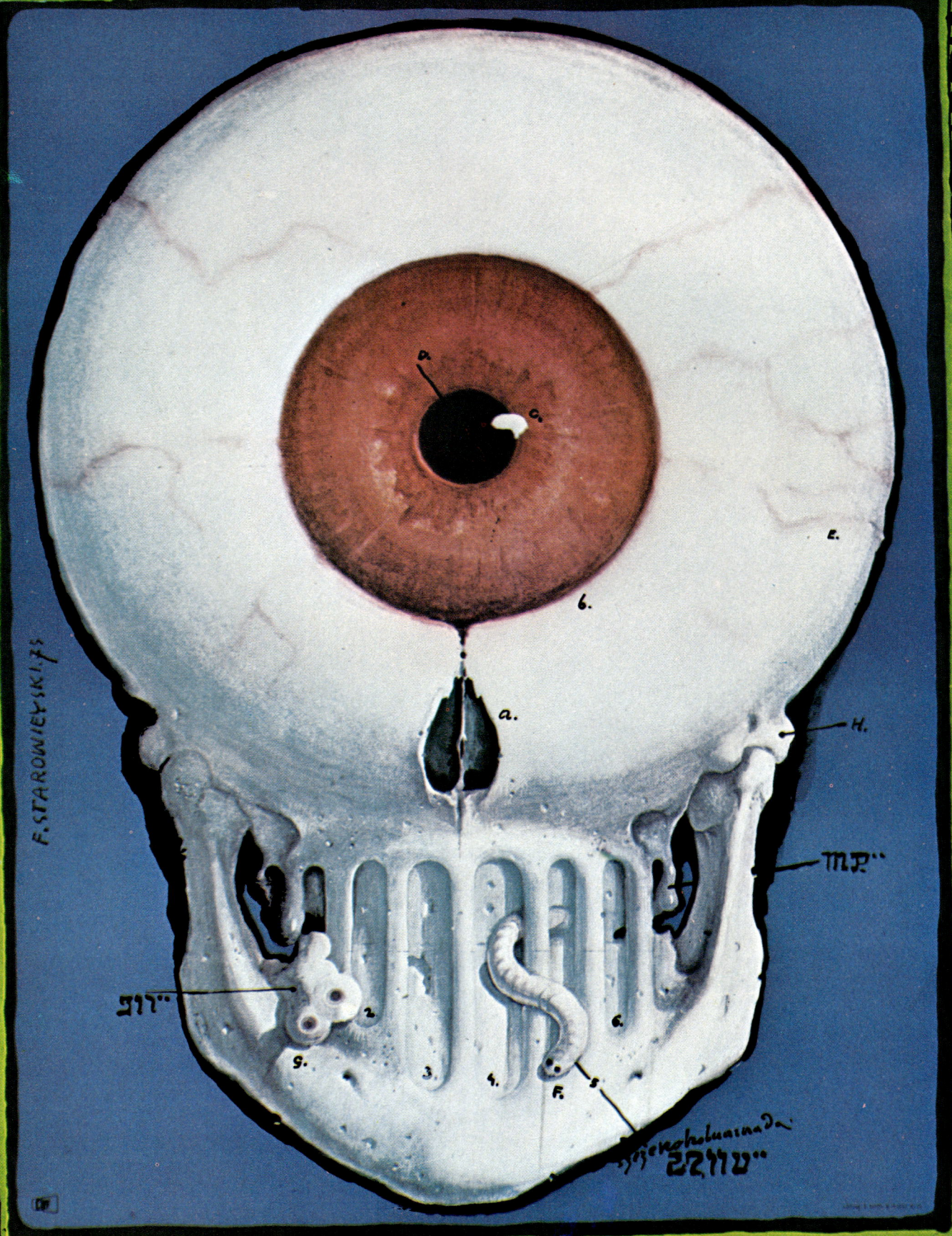

28 **Franciszek Starowieyski:** the film *The Sandglass Sanatorium* (1973)

29 **Franciszek Starowieyski:** the play *The Wedding* (1975)

30 **Waldemar Świerzy:** the play *The Lady from Maxim's* (1968)

Thirteenth
International
Festival
of Contemporary
Music

WARSAW
AUTUMN
WARSAW 20 — 28 SEPTEMBER 1969

31 Waldemar Świerzy: music festival (1969)

CYRK

32   **Waldemar Świerzy:** circus (1971)

33   **Waldemar Świerzy:** circus (1972)

JIMI HENDRIX

34 **Waldemar Świerzy:** the singer Jimi Hendrix (1974)

35 Waldemar Świerzy: circus (1975)

36 **Henryk Tomaszewski:** the Belgian Secessionist poster (1973)

37   **Maciej Urbaniec:** circus (1970)

38 Maciej Urbaniec: the opera *Boris Godunov* (1972)

TOWARZYSTWO PRZYJACIÓŁ DZIECI

międzynarodowy dzień dziecka

39 **Maciej Urbaniec:** International Children's Day (1973)

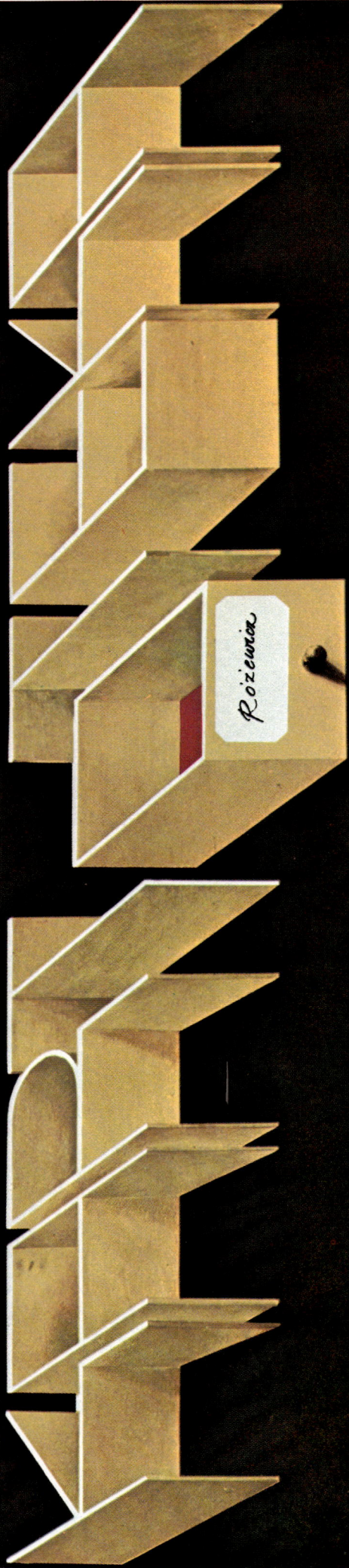

teatr maly

40 **Maciej Urbaniec:** the play *The File* (1975)

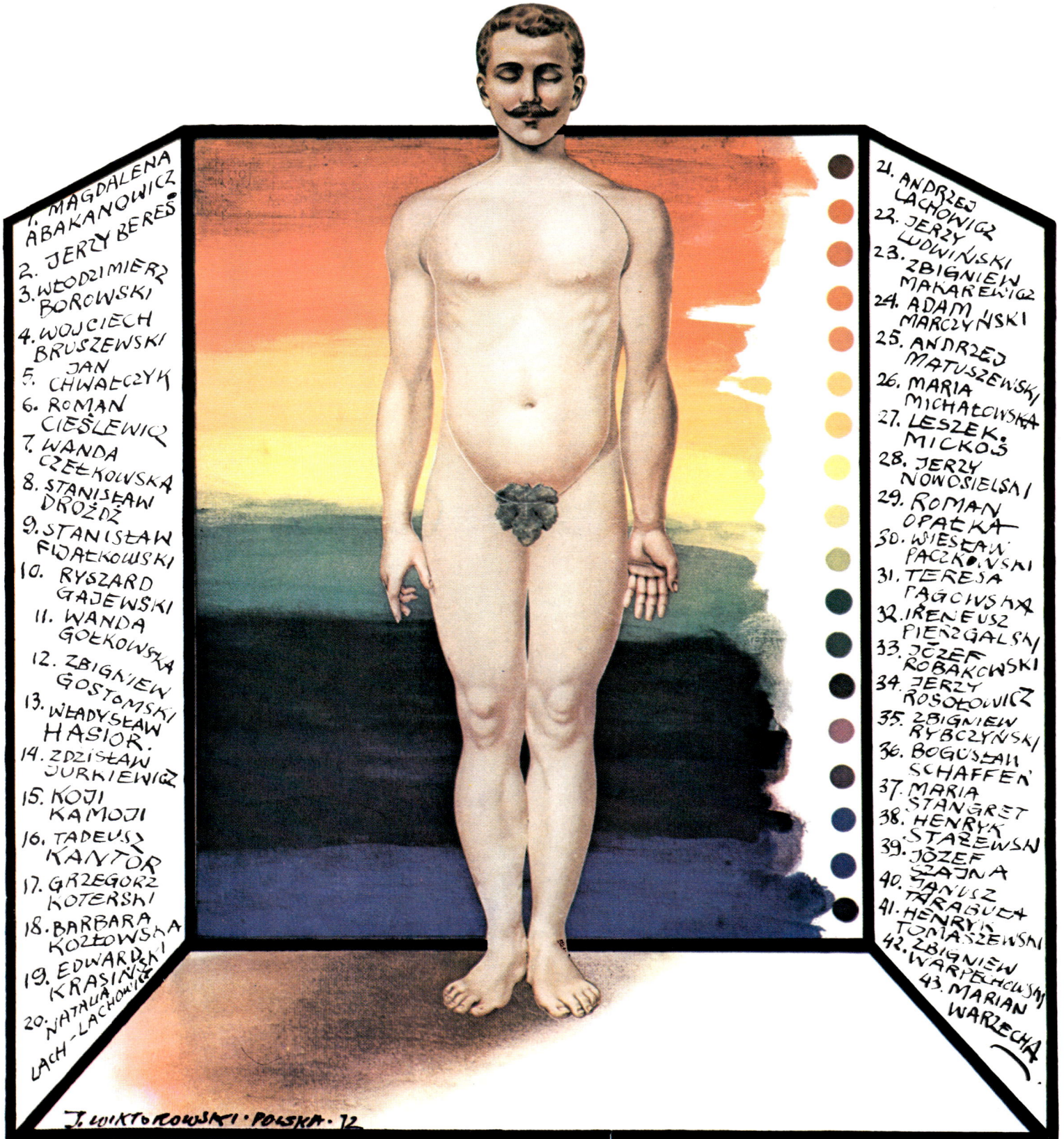

ATELIER 72
THE RICHARD DEMARCO GALLERY
8 MELVILLE CRESCENT EDINBURGH EH3 7NB

1. MAGDALENA ABAKANOWICZ
2. JERZY BEREŚ
3. WŁODZIMIERZ BOROWSKI
4. WOJCIECH BRUSZEWSKI
5. JAN CHWAŁCZYK
6. ROMAN CIEŚLEWICZ
7. WANDA CZEŁKOWSKA
8. STANISŁAW DROŻDŻ
9. STANISŁAW FIJAŁKOWSKI
10. RYSZARD GAJEWSKI
11. WANDA GOŁKOWSKA
12. ZBIGNIEW GOSTOMSKI
13. WŁADYSŁAW HASIOR
14. ZDZISŁAW JURKIEWICZ
15. KOJI KAMOJI
16. TADEUSZ KANTOR
17. GRZEGORZ KOTERSKI
18. BARBARA KOZŁOWSKA
19. EDWARD KRASIŃSKI
20. NATALIA LACH-LACHOWICZ

21. ANDRZEJ LACHOWICZ
22. JERZY LUDWIŃSKI
23. ZBIGNIEW MAKAREWICZ
24. ADAM MARCZYŃSKI
25. ANDRZEJ MATUSZEWSKI
26. MARIA MICHAŁOWSKA
27. LESZEK MICKOŚ
28. JERZY NOWOSIELSKI
29. ROMAN OPAŁKA
30. WIESŁAW PACZKOWSKI
31. TERESA PĄGOWSKA
32. IRENEUSZ PIERZGALSKI
33. JÓZEF ROBAKOWSKI
34. JERZY ROSOŁOWICZ
35. ZBIGNIEW RYBCZYŃSKI
36. BOGUSŁAW SCHAFFER
37. MARIA STANGRET
38. HENRYK STAŻEWSKI
39. JÓZEF SZAJNA
40. JANUSZ TARABUŁA
41. HENRYK TOMASZEWSKI
42. ZBIGNIEW WARPECHOWSKI
43. MARIAN WARZECHA

J. WIKTOROWSKI · POLSKA · 72

41 Janusz Wiktorowski: exhibition of Polish art (1972)

42 Danuta Żukowska: circus (1970)